SAVED in Stilettos

21 Days To

✝ FAITH
✝ FASHION
✝ FABULOUS

AMITRICE LOWE

motique media

Publishing division of Motique Momentums, LLC

www.danielaGabrielle.com

ISBN: 0692250166
ISBN-13: 9780692250167

DEDICATION

With a loving heart, I dedicate

SAVED *in* **Stilettos**

to:

My Heavenly Father

Thanks for trusting me enough to deliver a message to Your people. I never dreamed or thought of being an author. Saved In Stilettos was an unplanned spiritual pregnancy and God, in His infinite wisdom, used me to birth a movement. I am eternally grateful!

The two loves of my life, Antonese and AJ

Thank you for honoring me and being such awesome children. I am so blessed that God allowed me to be your mother. Saved In Stilettos is only the beginning of the legacy that I will leave for you. I declare that I will do all I can to position you for greatness! Mama loves you 2 dearly.

My mom, Mrs. Janice Lowe

.... your people *shall be* my people, and your God, my God! Mom, thanks for being a woman of great Faith. Since birth you have instilled the Love of God in me and now knowing Him for myself I see that I am so blessed to have a God fearing mom. I am the woman that I am today because of you and your loving guidance. Mom, you have always been my biggest supporter and my biggest fan. You loved me even when I was not loveable, Thanks. I love and appreciate you!

My entire family

Thanks for being so loving and supportive!

My Spiritual Father, the overseer of my soul, Pastor De"Quin"drae Hardnett, Lady D and the New Destiny Church family

Thank you! A few years ago I walked into New Destiny Church with an Abrahamic type call facing the unknown and you all embraced me. Pastor Quin, I can't thank you enough for being the man of God and a great teacher. Leading by example, you motivate and challenge me to be better, Thanks!

CONTENTS

INTRODUTION.....*Girl Talk*

WEEK ONE

WEEK TWO

WEEK THREE

FOREWORD

There's something about a fierce pair of stilettos that gives a woman the confidence and boldness to conquer the world. Whether red, pink, studded or peep-toed, every woman has a favorite pair. What happens when we wear our salvation like our favorite high heel? Where would our lives be when we strut in purpose and destiny like we do in those fabulous high heels?

This is the time and the season to go full speed ahead into the plan that God has for your life. Whether in the boardroom or the classroom, in the home or on the playground, you have been destined to walk in marvelous places. There is a high call to transform the world around you. This is your hour to move. **What are you waiting for?**

Regardless of what you've been told there is a completely EXTRAORDINARRY woman in you that loves God and looks great doing it. You don't have to loose who you are to be in love with Him. The truth is that in Him you will find a beauty that cannot be explained only experienced.

Saved In Stilettos is a twenty-one day catalyst to purpose. Get ready to have your walk with God ignited in a way you have never experienced. It will draw you closer in relationship with God while stirring every gift that's inside of you. Take the journey inward and watch what happens outward. You'll weep, laugh and identify with these fabulously faith-filled women who have paved the way for us as Christian women to be fashionable, fierce, faith-filled and ultimately fabulous.

Daniela Gabrielle
Best Selling Author of Fly Free: Finding the Courage to Live Without Limitations & Big Mouth Big Dreams
Orlando, Florida
www.danielaGabrielle.com

INTRODUCTION

Girl Talk

As a little girl, I sat on the back pew of the church and I can vividly remember seeing the women wearing sequin and rhinestone dresses parading down the aisle. The dresses were accessorized with hats, BIG hats. Not just ordinary hats but colorful, glittery hats that were coupled with beads, flowers and feathers. Sometimes so big that they would block my view! They would step high in their coordinating pumps that stood tall and showed off their opaque colored stockings. The Bible in one hand and their purse in the other, they were ready for "Sunday go to meeting" (as my father often called it). I can remember looking in admiration thinking, "I love it, they are simply gorgeous!"

After I grew up and became a mom myself I tried to keep with the same tradition, but my daughter was not feeling this "dressing up for church thing." Saturday nights would be chaotic!

Dresses, shiny patent leather shoes and white tights would be all over her room as she tried on dress after dress to determine what she would wear the next day for church. Sunday mornings were filled with uncontrollable tears and anger because she "hated", in her words, what she had to wear. Clearly, picking out clothing and fussing about what she can and cannot wear became the focus instead of going to worship God. Finally, I got to a place where I said clothing is not worth me losing my witness with my daughter! If she is clean and decent then she can wear it.

Following the voice of God, I transitioned to a church where the culture was much different. The pastor often teaches that the focus is on souls, not clothes. This became evident in my church when on Easter Sunday we wore jeans and t-shirts so no one would feel like they were left out. They didn't want any person to not come to church because they did not have a new Easter dress or suit. I soon learned the trend for church wear was changing. This made me begin to ponder,

👠 Do I have to wear stockings every Sunday

🔖 If I don't wear stockings, am I less anointed?

🔖 Is it okay for me to wear jeans to church on a Sunday?"

The thoughts that plagued my mind over the years were now becoming clear to me as I came into a deeper relationship with God. I learned that God was anointing me even in my jeans and that I (as well as you) can be saved and wear stilettos!

Do not take this as an excuse to break out your tight miniskirts, strapless halters and short shorts to church because there is a standard! We are women of God and we should always carry ourselves in a way that edifies His name. I'm imparting to you that what is on the inside will manifest on the outside so once we become whole with who God has called us to be then we can live a Faithful, Fashionable and Fabulous life in Him.

Proverbs is the book of wisdom. It provides practical wisdom for answers to day to day issues.

Proverbs 31 speaks to the
virtues that are in you.

Proverbs 31 speaks to the

Faithful and Fabulous

YOU!

Proverbs 31 starts off (verses 1-9) with a mother speaking to her son, King Leumel (little is known about him other than his name means devoted to God). In the introduction, the first nine verses of Proverbs 31, the mother discourages her son from living a life of ungodly behavior. As she goes in-depth into imparting her mother's wit, King Lemuel's mother begins to teach him the characteristics of the type of woman he should seek after as his wife. The 10th verse the passage begins to describe what has become commonly known as the Virtuous Woman. Let's take a look at what Proverbs Divine author, the Holy Spirit ("All Scripture is inspired by God and profitable for teaching, for reproof, for correction, for training in righteousness"- 2 Timothy 3:16), meant for His fabulous daughters.

Saved in Stilettos is the book for the woman that wants it all and YOU determine what ALL is for YOU! Whether married or single, with or without children, working or staying at home this book is for YOU! It seeks to serve as a guide to help you live a virtuous life that benefits you and everyone you encounter. Proverbs 31 speaks life into the very essence of who you are as a daughter of the King.

With your stilettos standing tall, grab your favorite pen, this book and meet me for a standing morning coffee break as we take this 21-day journey together. If you are a part of a women's ministry or book club, you can even make it a "Skinny Jeans and Stilettos" girl's night out as you redefine your relationship with God. I would love to take this journey with you and your "girls!"

However you chose to take this journey, I want you to read about the heart of these women of the Bible while relating it to your life. What can you learn from her? How can what she did or who she was increase your faith to become a more fabulous you in God? In other words, how can you take this and apply it to your life and your current/future situations to help yourself and others?

Let this journey inspire you to move into a season of greater for your life. You were destined to walk in high places…let's take a walk on the faith-filled fabulous side of life!

WEEK ONE

"Fashion fades, only style
remains the same."
-Coco Chanel

AMITRICE LOWE

DAY ONE

Are Diamonds Really a Girls Best Friend?

"A wife of noble character who can find? She is
worth far more than rubies."
Proverbs 31:10 (KJV)

In the early 90's Janet Jackson came out with a
hit pop song called Diamonds where she boldly
asked "Don't you know diamonds are a girl's best
friend?" I'm sure that many of us ladies can agree
a carat or two, especially coupled with a nice
French manicure definitely wouldn't make our
hand look *that* bad! However, here in Proverbs
31 it speaks of the type of woman that God
intends for us to be. In the message version of
this scripture it says the Proverbs 31 woman's
worth is far more than diamonds and the New
American Standard Bible translation states more
than jewels.

Simply put…

Girlfriend…

you are **WORTHY!**

God has appraised your value as **PRICELESS**

So, if a woman's worth exceeds the finest of jewels, are diamonds a girl's best friend or is the worth of a woman a man's best friend?

Proverbs 31:10 speaks of a "wife" of noble character, my dearest sister, the first marriage that you should have is a Spiritual one. The marriage should take place between you and God. Your heart should be in covenant with His. Being married to Him first is vital in understanding your worth. Your worth outweighs the finest of jewels and precious stones. As a Godly woman, you are a treasure and should be sought after.

In hanging out with some teenage girls recently, I was informed that the young lady's friend approached a young man in an attempt to hook the young lady up with this young man. She gave the young man her friend's phone number in hopes that he would call her friend. I quickly told the young ladies about the scripture above. I went on to boldly proclaim, "Although you are not ready for marriage right now, you need to understand that as the woman, you are the prize to be sought after." As she looked at me I went on to paint this picture for her. When gamblers play the Mega Millions lottery, the lottery tickets do not get out of the machine and chase after or beg people to buy them. People stand in long lines and spend lots of money in hopes of winning the prize. In other words, they chase the prize; the prize does not chase them. God deemed you so worthy, yeah you, that a man has to seek Him to have you as his wife.

My dear sister, know your value! If he is not your husband, he is not worthy of husband benefits. In other words, get him out of your bed and send that joker home until he puts a ring on it. If you are married, remember that you are still valuable and your life brings a wealth of treasure to your home. Just like a diamond is regularly reappraised, as women, you grow in value as you grow in God. The more you surrender to the plan of God for your life, the more your value increases. Make sure you are being kept spiritually, emotionally and physically. You are worth the investment.

fASH∩ONIsTa
PROFILE

EVE
Genesis 2:22

God saw that it was not good for man to be alone so he put Adam to sleep and made Eve. Ladies, take note here of how our daddy feels about us. Before God made Eve He made sure the man, Adam, had a place to stay and means to take care of her. God brought Eve on the scene once he knew that Adam was in a place to provide for her. God deemed women as a compliment to a man. This is complimentary, sort of like you have the perfect pair of red stilettos to go with your little black dress, it just works. He made us, to help birth greatness. God placed something on the inside of you that enables you to birth greatness out of any situation.

Often times we put a negative connation to Eve because she sinned, but we must honor her for who God made her to be. Eve birthed greatness both naturally and spiritually. Let's face it Eve birthed great lessons for the women who came behind her. Eve was made for a special purpose, to compliment man and to give birth. Even though Eve sinned, this did not take away the fact that God still covered her. This is much like us. We don't always get it right but when we repent God's grace and love covers us through His son Christ Jesus!

ACCESSORIZE
YOUR FAITH

🥾 What are your feelings of self worth?

_____

_____

_____

_____

🥾 Whether married or single, do you feel as
though you are a treasure to be sought
after?

_____

_____

_____

_____

🔖 Do you allow your mistakes to dictate who you are in Christ?

_____

_____

_____

_____

fABuLoUs
FAITH
Time

In your Fabulous "FAITH" Time with God I encourage you to get in His presence. Ask him what feelings of unworthiness or inadequacies you may be dealing with. Ask Him to reveal a plan to help you overcome those feelings.

My Fabulous sister, remember you are made to compliment and to walk into a situation, heels standing tall and boldly declare greatness into any situation. You are *Fearfully and Wonderfully* made!

AMITRICE LOWE

DAY TWO

Salvation Over Stilettos

"The heart of her husband safely trusts her; So he
will have no lack of gain."
Proverbs 31:10

I can still hear feet stomping, hand clapping,
praying deacons singing, I'm so glad salvation is
free; FREE for you and me. I now understand
that though salvation was not free for Jesus,
(actually it cost Him His life) the hymnist was
correct in that Salvation is free for you and me
girlfriend! About six years ago God began to
purge me of religion and tradition and called me
into relationship with Him. I was terrified!!!! He
was separating me from all I ever knew and
calling me to the unfamiliar. During this time I
sought out wise counsel from my Spiritual

mentor, Sis. Cynetha Williams. She explained to me that God was purging me to prepare me for my purpose in Him. She went on to speak His word into my life and left me with these powerful words,

"God has to be able to TRUST YOU!"

As I mentioned earlier your first marriage is to be in covenant with Christ and He has to be able to trust you to be about His business.

Our steps are ordered by God and salvation is the first step in your faith walk. Whether you are walking in 6-inch spiked stilettos or all black classic 4-inch heels the goal is to keep walking by faith. Once you are saved, allow God to lead you beyond the surface and get into a more intimate relationship with Christ. It is your intimacy with Christ and obedience to His will that builds trust along the way.

fASHIONIsTa
PROFILE

PRICILLA

Acts 18:18-28

Pricilla was a woman of the Word that understood how to work the word to impact the world. Her husband, Aquila, trusted her and she helped her husband teach the Gospel of Jesus Christ. Her husband knew that she was saved and was able to teach the Word of God and help him lead people to Jesus Christ. Priscilla, along with her husband, was instrumental in walking Apollos, a Biblical teacher, into the truth of the crucified, risen and glorified Savior, in other words the true Salvation. Before she could do this, God had to know He could trust that she wouldn't get jealous of Apollos teaching and try to discredit his walk with God. Likewise, God needs to know that you and I are trustworthy and do not operate based on our own motives and agenda.

✝AcCEßSoRIzE
Y O U R   F A I T H

🥿 Are you SAVED? _____

🥿 Again, do you know for sure that are you Saved?

_____

_____

_____

🥿 If you are not Saved, let get you Saved! If you are Saved can He trust you with His assignment?

_____

_____

_____

In your Fabulous "FAITH" Time with God I encourage you to get in His presence. So many times we join church because that's what mama and grandmamma said for us to do. So we join the church, but our Salvation is not certain. Salvation is a confession of the mouth and a true act of the heart.

Prayer of Salvation

If you are not saved confess this prayer out loud:

I come to you in the name of Jesus. I acknowledge to You that I am a sinner and I need your forgiveness. I believe that your only begotten son Jesus Christ died for my sins and I am now willing to turn from my sins. You said in Your Holy Word, Romans 10:9, that if we confess the Lord our God and believe in our hearts that God raised Jesus from the dead, we shall be saved. Right now I confess Jesus as the Lord of my soul. With my heart, I believe that God raised Jesus from the dead. This very moment I accept Jesus Christ as my own personal Savior and according to His Word, right now I am saved.

In Jesus name. Amen.

DAY THREE

The Real Housewives of the Bible

"She does him good and not evil all the days of her life"
Proverbs 31:12

A few years ago there was a popular reality series that started to come on television. The Real Housewives franchise quickly became a household hit among reality TV fans. The funny thing about the show was that many of the housewives were not actually wives. This was profound to me and God showed me this concept from a spiritual prospective. God has placed something in us women to take something ordinary and make it EXTRAORDINARY. Although many criticized the "wives" without husbands, here is the truth. Although you may not be a wife in the natural, you still possess the ability make a house a home.

What many may not know is that even though this show may have started only a few years ago, the Real Housewives concept dates back to the Bible days. When you think of a wife, in essence all wives are housewives. We all care, nurture, and cultivate the home in a way that can bring joy and prosperity into our family's life. The only difference is that some wives also work outside the home.

There's no dividing line between the "fabulousness" that is a woman. Whether you work inside the home or outside the home, whether you are married or single, as a fabulous, fierce and faith-filled woman you are commissioned as a woman of God to take care of the home. Your role is to set the atmosphere in your home so that it conducive to positive growth. Taking care of the home is not only about house cleaning and décor, it is creating an environment that becomes an incubator for the gifts that God has placed inside of you and your household to develop and manifest.

Don't be afraid of the label "Housewife." It's a

badge of honor that says you, girlfriend, can turn a house into a home, a vision into a victory, a story into a storage container of blessings.

The Real Housewives of the Bible consists of a lengthy cast; so let's just talk about a good wife, Abigail and an evil wife, Jezebel.

fASHIONIsTa
PROFILE

ABIGAIL

1 Samuel 25

Abaigail, could be considered the fashion designer of a much needed wardrobe must-have, Humility! Humbly submitting yourself to your husband clearly puts you in a trustworthy position in his eyes.

Abaigail, in humility, pleaded to King David and as a result saved her husband's household from destruction. Because of her humility and wisdom Abigail not only preserved the men of her household but she eventually became David's wife.

My fabulous sister, do not look at your wardrobe in just the physical sense, but what you are wearing in the spiritual realm. One thing that we can probably agree on as women is that most of us CANNOT go without earrings. One of my friends says "Amitrice, no earrings, you are in a clear violation of the fashion code. Even my pastor's nine-year old daughter knows earrings are a fashion must have. When she spots me without earrings she greets me with "Ms. Amitrice, where are your earrings?" Likewise, a lack of humility is a violation! Make sure you are clothed in humility.

JEZEBEL
1 Samuel 25

Evil, manipulative, and controlling are three words to describe the evil wife of Ahab. Jezebel used her influence as a wife for evil. She used her controlling and manipulative ways to convince her husband to do evil. Eventually they both died. Since then Jezebel's name has been synonymous with evil.

Now, as we talk I can see you saying, "That's not me." Well actually if you are exposed to the spirit of Jezebel you can fall prey to it before you know it and because it is such a strong spirit you will not even recognize what you are doing.

🥿 Think about how you react with others, do you think you are operating in good or evil?

_____

_____

_____

🥿 Do you bow in humility when interacting with others? Or is it your way or no way? Do you have to be in control of everything?

_____

_____

_____

Do you use manipulative tactics to get your

way?_____

_____

_____

fABuLOUs
FAITH
Time

In your Fabulous "FAITH" Time with God I encourage you to get in His presence. Ask God to show you, YOU! Take a look in the mirror. Ask God to reveal to you the areas in your life that need to be worked on. Ask God to show you if you are operating in His Spirit or an evil Spirit. Just remember you must be ready to see what He may reveal.

_____
_____
_____
_____
_____
_____
_____
_____
_____
_____
_____
_____
_____
_____
_____
_____
_____
_____
_____

DAY FOUR
Project Runway

She looks for wool and flax And works with her
hands in delight
Proverbs 31:13 (NASB)

Sewing is an age-old craft that dates back to the
bible days. Women mostly made clothing and
fine garments. Today we do not see as many
seamstresses as we did in the biblical days or
should I say we have them we just called them a
different name. Now they are called fashion
designers. Project Runway is a reality show where
designers compete to design the best runway
fashions. On the show, the contestants have very
limited materials and have to create a design with
limited resources; however most of them find
great joy in designing fashion for their models.

Likewise, women in the bible found delight in

making clothing for their family and sometimes for the priests. I know now and days many of us are not sewing and making our own clothes, but we as women do shop to buy clothing for our own families. This is a commonality between many women. We sometimes plan special days and events just to have a girls shopping trip. This let us know that we find delight in it.

fAs**h**uoNIsTa
PROFILE

THE WOMEN OF EXODUS 35

Exodus 35:25-26

"All the women who were skilled in sewing and spinning prepared blue, purple, and scarlet yarn, and fine linen cloth, and they brought them in." Exodus 35:25. The Women of Exodus 35 used their skill and talent for the Kingdom of God.

Now in modern day times you would see the name of these women in the fashion magazine describes as the stylist to the stars. These women did it for a Kingdom purpose and they did it with a cheerful heart!

They came together for a common good. When we work and give of our talent with a cheerful heart it pleases God. These women used the talent they had for the up building of God's kingdom.

ACCESSORIZE
YOUR FAITH

🥿 Do you serve/give in ministry?

_____

_____

_____

🥿 What are your motives for serving/giving of your time and talent? Are they pure?

_____

_____

_____

🥿 Are there areas you think you could do more?

_____

_____

fABuLOUs
FAITH
Time

Get in the presence of God and ask Him to show you the motives behind your actions. Ask God to show you how and where He wants you to work and give in ministry. Ask Him to help you work and give as if you were doing it only for Him. Working unto the Lord avoids burn out and the feeling of being overwhelmed.

DAY FIVE

Passport to Greatness

"She is like merchant ships; She brings her food from afar."
Proverbs 31:14 (NASB)

What you feed will grow. Just as a baby eats and grows, we in the Body of Christ must do the same thing. In order to maintain healthy lives it is our responsibility to ensure that we are eating, both physically and spiritually. Merchant ships travel around the world bringing different things back to the shore. One version of the Bible even states she brought back exotic things, things that would not be found in your familiar everyday surroundings. As a woman saved in stilettos and walking the Faith, you can't be afraid to travel to get what you need for yourself and your family.

You must be willing, even if you have to go abroad, to get the food we need to nourish your spiritual, emotional, intellectual and emotional growth. Conferences, business meetings, seminars, programs whatever you need to become a better you, Go get it!

fAS*h*IoNIsTa
PROFILE

RUTH

The Book of Ruth

Ruth, led by her mentor & mother in love, Naomi, traveled from the land of Moab to be able to have food and the necessities to survive after the death of their spouses. Notice in the book of Ruth, originally both Opal and Ruth were with Naomi. Along the journey, Opal went back to what was familiar to her.

Girl, sometimes you will have to leave some people and some things behind to get to your destiny! After her journey, Ruth and Naomi arrived in Judah. Ruth worked hard daily and brought food home for her family. Ruth did not wait for a handout; she got up and worked for it.

God knew the plan He had for Ruth. He just wanted to see if she was willing to listen to the wise council He had place in her life. (Girl, notice I say wise council, do not except council from just anybody). Once He saw Ruth's obedience he sent provision for her, Boaz.

Sometimes our passport to greatness is outside of our comfort zone. You have to be willing to travel into a new place spiritually, emotionally and physically to receive your Boaz. Boaz is a representation of the provision God has prepared for our lives in alignment with destiny. When your back is up against the wall, know that in you are the tools and resources needed to sustain you. Ruth lost her husband. I could only imagine the pain of loosing a spouse. While I'm sure she mourned loosing her best friend, the truth was she also lost her provider. In her obedience to follow Naomi she discovered provision. You may have lost your job, your spouse, your friends or some other form of security and stability in your life, but this is not the time to be discouraged. Don't curse the death of an old provider, God is here and he wants to remind you that HE WILL PROVIDE.

ACCESSORIZE
YOUR FAITH

🥿 What things are you feeding in your life?

_____
_____
_____

🥿 Are you taking the proper steps to ensure that you and your family are being fed spiritually?_____

_____

_____

🥿 Are you willing to work at becoming a better woman of God or do you feel it should just come to you? _____

_____

_____

fABuLOUs
FAITH
Time

In your Fabulous "FAITH" Time with God I encourage you to get in His presence. Ask God are you starving spiritually? Ask Him to show you what to do, where to go and how to get to a place of spiritual nourishment. Seek Him to show you the people you need in your life to help you grow spiritually.

DAY SIX
Upgrade Your Shoe Game

"She rises also while it is still night And gives food to her household And portions to her maidens"
Proverbs 31:15 (NASB)

Upgrade, Upsize and Update are common words we hear in our day-to-day dealings. From "would you like to upsize your order?" in the drive thru to upgrading to the latest and best tech gadget, let's face it ladies, upgrading is the new "it factor."

We are on a constant move to make things better. Like the Proverbs woman, we arise early enough to spend time with our Heavenly Father and then prepare our day for our families and communities. In this passage, rising while it is still night represents that the Proverbs Woman is consistently thinking of, and helping others.

If you are not up on your game and elevating to the next level in God, you are not rising while it is night and this is a cause for an upgrade. You have to change your thought process. Begin to arise early enough to mediate on God's Word and you will begin to see that you are rising to the next level in your Faith walk.

fAS**h**ONI**s**Ta
PROFILE

THE WIDOW OF ZAREPHATH
1 Kings 17:7-24

When Elisha came into contact with the Widow of Zarephath she was wearing defeat while walking into a dark pit of death. The Widow and her son had very little food to eat so she made up in her mind that she was going to feed them one last time and then they both would die. Thank God, God had another plan.

While the woman is preparing to stare death in the face, here's God in the heaven orchestrating her breakthrough through someone else. God speaks to the heart of the prophet Elisha and instructs him to go to the woman to get food.

The prophet gets there and tells the woman to feed him. Now can't you see this woman, who barely has enough food to feed her and her child, look at him like "REALLY?! So let me get this right. You want me to take food out of our mouth to feed you?

Listen closely my sister because this is a teachable moment: The widow did NOT let flesh over ride her decision to hear from God by way of the prophet. An upgrade in the Widow's thinking put her in position to NEVER be hungry again.

✝ACCESSORIZE
Y O U R   F A I T H

🥿 Does your thinking need an upgrade? Are you in a place to receive a Word from the prophet Or will you ignore it based on your circumstance?

_____

_____

_____

🥿 Are you in a place where you are down to your last and you feel defeated?

_____

_____

_____

🥿 Are you making decision out of the flesh or are you listening to the Holy Spirit?

_____

_____

_____

fABuLOUs
FAITH
Time

In your Fabulous "FAITH" Time with God I encourage you to get in His presence. I can only imagine that Elijah was probably not freshly dressed after traveling. So what if the widow, like many of us look at Elijah outside appearance and ignored the message he had for her?

DAY SEVEN
Sewing In Stilettos

"She considers a [new] field before she buys *or* accepts it [expanding prudently and not courting neglect of her present duties by assuming other duties]; with her savings [of time and strength] she plants fruitful vines in her vineyard."

Proverbs 31:16 (AMP)

According to dictionary.com, to invest is to put (money) to use, by purchase or expenditure, in something offering potential profitable returns, as interest, income, or appreciation in value. An investor is someone who invests money to use with the potential of a profitable return or in terms of the scripture produce some fruit. Usually before investing the risk of the investment is considered to determine whether there will be a positive return of funding. Good investors are the ones that know "when to hold'em and when to fold'em".

As women of God you have to be willing to sow into your footsteps & invest in yourself! My sister we have to stop investing so much of our money, time and talent in things that depreciate in value! Invest in and sow in fertile soil, things you know that will yield you a fruitful return. We must understand the law of sowing and reaping. When we sow God answers are YES and AMEN because He has promised in His Word to give seed to the sower and a plentiful harvest.

fAS**h**IONIsTa
PROFILE

THE SHUNAMMITE WOMAN
2 Kings 4:8-37

The scripture tells us that the Shunammite woman was wealthy. When Elisha would pass by her house this woman would feed Elisha. The Shunammite woman knew that Elisha was a man of God and wanted to prepare a place for him to eat and rest when he came through her town.

Take heed to what the Shunammite does. She said to her husband, "I am sure this man who stops in from time to time is a holy man of God. Let's build a small room for him on the roof and furnish it with a bed, a table, a chair, and a lamp. Then he will have a place to stay whenever he comes by." Even though the scripture says in 2 Kings 4:8 this woman was wealthy she still respected her marriage and submitted to her husband. She did not take on the "it's my money and I can do what I want to with it" type attitude. She deemed it necessary to go to her husband to get the okay (acknowledge).

The Shunammite woman made an investment in Elisha and in return God gave her a son. Not only did He give her a son, but he allowed her son to later be brought back to life by the Prophet she invested in.

✝ACCESSORIZE
YOUR FAITH

👠 What are some of the things you consider
   when making an investment?

   _____

   _____

   _____

👠 Are you investing in yourself?

   _____

   _____

   _____

♥ Are you making wise investments in your Spiritual life and in your finances?

_____

_____

_____

♥ Are your investments producing fruit? Are you reaping a harvest?

_____

_____

_____

fABuLoUs
FAITH
Time

In your Fabulous "FAITH" Time with God I encourage you to get in His presence. Ask God to help you to make wise investments. Ask God to help you to acknowledge Him and not allow you to lean to your own understanding.

WEEK TWO

"The most important thing to remember is that you can wear all the greatest clothes and all the greatest shoes, but you've got to have a good spirit on the inside. That's what's really going to make you look like you're ready to rock the world."
-Alicia Keys

AMITRICE LOWE

DAY EIGHT
Strength Looks Good on You

"She girds herself with strength And makes her arms strong"

Proverbs 31:17 (NASB)

Two months after obtaining my undergraduate degree I started to work in Corporate America at a Fortune 500 company. The corporate executives would come in the room with their designer suits and dresses looking like they had stepped off the cover of the latest fashion magazine.

Fashion was part of their corporate culture. As one of the top-level managers addressed us, I remember looking at her like, "WOW! She has it all together!" Her hair was flawlessly layered in a bouncing bob, her tailored made suit screamed power and her shoes, well just say they look like they would be on the runway. The girl was BAD, in a good kind of way.

As she addressed the new employees that were hungry for success, one thing she said stood out. She boldly proclaimed, "Dress for the job you want, not for the job you are in!" That day she taught us a valuable lesson in leadership, what you wear can affect where you go.

In the scripture referenced above, the word gird in the Hebrew means to prepare or to put on. A vital part of the virtuous woman's wardrobe is strength. Daily she puts on the whole armor of God. Ephesians 6:10-11 tells us to be strong in the Lord and in his mighty power. Put on all of God's armor so that you will be able to stand firm against all strategies of the devil. My friend this is not the type of thing that you can go to the nearest mall and buy but it's something that comes from within, the joy of the Lord is our strength!

fAS*h*IoNI*s*Ta
PROFILE

YOU
Proverbs 31:17

Girl, where did you get that? What size is it? Do they have anymore and where can I get that look? God has poured out His Spirit of strength on you! Strength looks good on you, yep real good! Dressing the part is what you do my sister. You make sure that you are well prepared to play the game all while looking good.

Over the last seven days, we've looked at everyone else in the Bible, but just like the other Fashionista Profiles, you have your own story of how God has fashioned your faith and transformed your life.

Today I want you to pause and acknowledge your own personal story of strength. Celebrate the victories that God has brought in your life. Recognize that not only should you be dressed with strength today, but that you've been accessorized with it throughout your lifetime.

ACCESSORIZE
Y O U R   F A I T H

🥿 Are you operating in God's strength or your own?

_____

_____

_____

🥿 What are ways you ensure that you are remaining strong in the Lord?

_____

_____

_____

_____

🥿 Can you identify certain people/places/ things that make you weak? What do you do to avoid them/it?

_____

_____

_____

_____

fABuLOUs
FAITH
Time

In your Fabulous "FAITH" Time with God I encourage you to get in His presence. Ask God to show you how to operate in His strength and not your own. Ask God to show you ways to increasing your strength in and through Him.

_____
_____
_____
_____
_____
_____
_____
_____
_____
_____
_____
_____
_____
_____
_____
_____
_____
_____
_____
_____
_____

DAY NINE

How Much Does Your Oil Cost?

"She tastes *and* sees that her gain from work [with and for God] is good; her lamp goes not out, but it burns on continually through the night [of trouble, privation, or sorrow, warning away fear, doubt, and distrust]."

Proverbs 31:18 (AMP)

There is a parable in the Bible about ten virgins and their oil. In these times oil was used to fuel lamps for light. By using the oil, no matter what came, storm or rain, the light did not go out when the lamp was adequately fueled. In your life it is vital that you stay stored up with oil. It holds great value and sustains your personal lamp, which is your light in a dark world.

Getting into the presence of God refuels and restores your oil. It is the place where the oil flows freely to do the very things you have been gifted to do. The powerful thing about the oil is that it has the potential for unlimited flow in your life it you are willing to let it be released over your life. There is a cycle of outpouring that you need to embrace in your life. God pours into you in the secret place and then you pour out what He's placed in you whether it's a gift, talent; an extension of grace, an act of mercy or love, or a word of encouragement where He leads you to pour. As you pour out what He pours in, He will faithfully keep your lamp full.

In the word of God, oil was also used as a sign of restoration or anointing in ceremony. It was used to call the "called out" out to do the work of the ministry. Kings, minstrels, leaders and great figures were anointed with oil as a symbol of the authority of God released to flow in their callings. David was anointed King; Samuel was anointed as a prophet and you, girlfriend, have been anointed to walk in high places.

Matthew 26:7 talks about the woman with the alabaster box who poured an expensive ointment on Jesus. Many did not understand the cost of what was in her box but she was willing to freely pour it on Jesus. She paid a price for the oil she was carrying, but she saw the value in her sacrifice. As you release your oil, see the value in your sacrifice. Know the price of your oil and let it be given where it is received.

With the high value of your oil, you must begin to evaluate where your oil is shared. Are you serving or working out of obligation? If you are doing it because your family, friends, church, and/or job asked you to do and you feel obligated then it's not good. We have to learn to say no if we are not led by God! He is the light of the world and if you glorify Him in all you do your light will never go dim. When you work unto God and not man no matter what the Glory of God will shine through you.

fAS*h*IONI*s*Ta
PROFILE

WOMAN WITH THE ALABASTER BOX
Matthew 26:7-13

They told her no! They told her not to waste her oil on Jesus because she could sale the oil for money to be used to give to the poor. However, her wanting to serve God outweighed her wanting to listen to man out of obligation. The woman with the Alabaster Box took the oil and poured it on Jesus and washed His feet with her tears, her hair and the oil. They told Jesus that she was a sinful woman and He shouldn't allow her to touch Him. Jesus forgave her sins teaching them that she acted out of love.

ACCESSoRIzE
YOUR FAITH

🥿 Are you doing things out of obligation?

_____
_____
_____
_____
_____

🥿 Are you giving you best to God?

_____

_____

_____

🥿 During the rough times is God light still shining through you or have you let life's circumstance dim or even blow out your light?

_____

_____

_____

fABuLOUs
FAITH
Time

In your Fabulous "FAITH" Time with God I encourage you to get in His presence. Ask God is He able to shine His light through you or are there some dark areas that need to be addressed?

DAY TEN
The "Hott" Homemaker

"She's skilled in the crafts of home and hearth,
diligent in homemaking"

Proverbs 31:19 (Message)

The Proverbs 31 woman takes great joy in her family and home. The word hearth is defined in Merrian Webster online dictionary as the home or creative center. The Proverbs 31 woman is not just concerned about what she wears, but also how she keeps her home.

My sister, we work so hard to be fashionable on the outside, but remember we should want our homes just as fashionable and decent. My mom always taught me that being clean is close to Godliness. God does not dwell in unclean places. So I ask you, what type of atmosphere do you want to create in your home? The Proverbs 31 Woman takes pride in making sure her home is furnished with love and honor.

As a homemaker, we transform our household to be conducive for peace, prosperity and productivity. Take a look at your home and ask yourself, "What atmosphere have a set in my home."

- Does it stir creativity?
- Is it tranquil?
- It is centered on family interaction?
- Is it welcoming to you and your guests?
- Can the love of God be felt?
- Do I look forward to coming home?

As you look at your home, define what your home should be to you and determine in your heart that your house will be filled with Jesus and an atmosphere that pleases him. Balance your "hotness" by making your home comfortable in the natural with a deep cleaning, home makeover and some decoration upgrades. Then fill it with God's presence through prayer and worship in the home.

fAS*h*IONI*s*Ta
PROFILE

MARTHA
Luke 10:38-42

Martha is known throughout history as a busy body. She was the one that prepared the home for the arrival of Jesus. She was busy working and making sure that the home was decent and everything was in order when Jesus arrived. Martha worked while her sister Mary soaked in the presence of Jesus. Mary sat at his feet and learned. Although Martha was correct in her concern with the affairs homemaking, she missed the opportunity to spend intimate time with Jesus. Sisters, this is why we must have radical balance! We have to prioritize the many hats so that we can fulfill our many obligations as women.

ACCESSORIZE
YOUR FAITH

Are you so busy preparing your home that you miss out of time to get in Jesus presence?

_____

_____

_____

🥿 Are you so busy doing the Lord's work that you forget about the LORD of the work?_____

_____

🥿 Are you so busy that you do not have time to sit at the feet of Jesus to rest and learn in His presence?

_____

_____

_____

fABuLoUs
FAITH
Time

In your Fabulous "FAITH" Time with God I encourage you to get in His presence. Ask God to help you to slow down so that you can sit at His feet and soak in His presence.

_____
_____
_____
_____
_____
_____
_____
_____
_____
_____
_____
_____
_____
_____
_____
_____
_____
_____
_____

DAY ELEVEN

Ladies, Hold on to Your Pearls

"She opens her arms to the poor and extends her
hands to the needy"
Proverbs 31:20

Pearls are considered a timeless classic and a
must have accessory for all women. When I was
an upcoming senior in high school I remember
pearls was a must have for my senior drape
portrait. Even now today most women will tell
you that a pair of pearls coupled with the little
black dress is a powerful fashion statement in
itself. Genuine pearls are rare and often require a
great deal of work to find due to the fact that
there have to be certain conditions for them to
form.

Knowing this, would you just toss genuine pearls
to anyone or anything? Better yet would you find
them and just toss them back into the ocean
floor? Probably not, because you know their
value! The scripture states, "Do not give what is

holy to dogs, and do not throw your pearls before swine, or they will trample them under their feet, and turn and tear you to pieces (Matthew 7:6)."

You, your time, and your gifts are precious, just as genuine pearls! You are Holy, a daughter of the King! I remember asking a friend of mine would she just throw her genuine $300 designer logo bag out to the trash. She quickly answered NO! The same thing applies when you give of yourself to undeserving people and or things. They will not appreciate it. Most importantly, they will not appreciate where it comes from. If she threw her bag in the trash can the trash surely will not say, "Ooooooooo that's Gucci!"

Everyone cannot appreciate valuables, especially when they don't have any understanding of it's worth. As faith-filled fabulous women, it's is out responsibility to know our own worth and be stewards over how we cast our pearls.

fAS*/*lONIsTa
PROFILE

DORCAS

Acts 9:36

Dorcas was a philanthropist. The Bible states that this woman was full of good works and charitable deeds. There was a believer in Joppa named Tabitha, which in Greek is Dorcas (Acts 9:36). She was always doing kind things for others and helping the poor. Dorcas was careful of when and who she casted her pearls to. She gave to those who would appreciate her gift. Hopefully my sister you are doing the same.

+ACCESSORIZE
Y O U R   F A I T H

Who are you casting your pearls to?

_____

_____

Are you constantly finding yourself giving to others only to leave drained and depleted?

_____

_____

_____

_____

🥿 Who is filling you back up when you are
imparting to others?

🥿 _____

_____

_____

fABuLOUs
FAITH
Time

In your Fabulous "FAITH" Time with God I encourage
you to get in His presence. Ask God to send the right
people in your life that honor and value you and your
gifts. Ask God to show you who He has ordained to be in
your life to pour into you.

DAY TWELVE

Fear Factor

"She doesn't worry about her family when it snows; their winter clothes are all mended and ready to wear"

Proverbs 31:21

Worry is to think about your problems or fears. This is not the type of worry where you wear your peep toe pumps but you walk outside and realize you need your snow boots with the fur. I am talking about when you are so worried about your fears that it is debilitating. In reality television there was a show called Fear Factor that dared contestants to face their fears. Upon completion of a mission they were advanced to the next level. If they were unable to face their fears and complete a mission they failed and ultimately lost the contest.

Have you ever been fearful of something or doing something? Better yet, have you ever been worried about the outcome of something because you know deep down inside you failed to plan properly and you were not prepared? I think we can all agree that we have been there at one time or another.

During my undergrad years, I partied a lot. I thought I could hang out all day, party all night, and not properly prepare for my studies. I can vividly recall walking in the classroom worried about an exam or assignment because I was not properly prepared. The solution to this was first trusting God and secondly properly planning and preparing to succeed.

I'm not just talking about a physical preparation, but there are times when you will have to consecrate yourself and get your Spirit man prepared for what you will face. Fear met with God and preparation, are an equation for overcoming. Don't let fear keep you from your next level. Choose to face it and walk into your new season!

fAS/UONIsTa
PROFILE

MRS. JOB

The Book of Job

Imagine as Mrs. Job had to endure the heartache and pain of losing not just one but also all of her children. In addition to that, she sat there day after day watching the man she loves deteriorate. Job's wife watched her husband lose everything, even his health. Job's wife is often criticized because she encouraged him to curse God and die.

Girlfriend, let's keep it real, we all have been in a place that we allow our worries to overtake us and we say or do things based on the flesh. This is what happened with Job's wife. Instead of preparing through sanctification and consecration, she worried and responded out of fear. When we are faced with similar situations we must cast all of our cares on God and hold to God's Word.

"When I am afraid, I will put my trust in You."

Psalms 56:3

✝ACCESSORIZE
YOUR FAITH

🥿 What fears are you worried about?

🥿 _____

_____

_____

🥿 Have your fears allowed you to react in a
way that is not pleasing unto God?

🥿 _____

_____

_____

_____

🥿 Now that you have identified your fears, will you trust God to help you face your fears?

🥿 _____

_____

_____

_____

fABuLOUs
FAITH
Time

In your Fabulous "FAITH" Time with God I encourage you to get in His presence. Get intimate with God and address your fears with Him. Ask God how do you plan and prepare for success. God already knows but He wants you to cast it on Him so He can guide you through this.

AMITRICE LOWE

DAY THIRTEEN
DIY Style

"She makes for herself coverlets, cushions, *and* rugs of tapestry. Her clothing is of linen, pure *and* fine, and of purple [such as that of which the clothing of the priests and the hallowed cloths of the temple were made]."

Proverbs 31:22 AMP

We are in a season in American culture where so many are opting to do things themselves. From entire television networks like DIY to online websites like Pinterest and YouTube there is a wave of people longing to discovering the gift that's on the inside of them to enhance their beauty, home and lives.

From Brazilian hair weaves and eyelashes to custom made clothes and shoes, we are in a "why pay someone when I can do it myself" season.

The Proverbs 31 woman knew a little something-something about doing it herself. She took the gifts that she had to not only bless her home but to create a living in the marketplace. She chose to max out her gifts to bring her household into prosperous living.

What gifts and talents do you possess that could bring your life to next level living? There's a DYI woman in you. Your DYI gift is that thing that when everything else falls apart, it brings resources to your home. It could be organization, it could be doing hair or maybe even fashion design, but whatever it is, it was meant to add value to our life and family. Your DYI may not be mine and mine may not be yours, but there IS something in you that both you and the world needs. Let your creativity run wild. Let your gifts run deep. Tap into your reservoir of skills to transform your life.

fAS*h*IoNIsTa
PROFILE

TABITHA

Acts 9:36

This girl is bad! She wears many hats and still finds time to think of others. She used her gifts to make others. The scripture tells us that this was one of those ladies that sewed robes for the priest in the bible days.

Now earlier we talked about how she gave to the needy. So she not only made robes for the priest but she also used her resources to help the needy.

ACCESSORIZE
Y O U R   F A I T H

- How many hats are you wearing? _____
- What are they?
- _____

  _____

- Are you using your gifts to give back to others?
- _____

  _____

  _____

How are you using your gifts for the Kingdom?

_____

_____

_____

fABuLoUs
FAITH
Time

In your Fabulous "FAITH" Time with God I encourage you to get in His presence. Press in and ask God how He wants you to use your gifts and who He wants you to give back to.

AMITRICE LOWE

DAY FOURTEEN

Let Me Upgrade You

"Her husband is respected at the city gate, where
he takes his seat among the elders of the land."

Proverbs 31:23

Whether it is Jackie Kennedy, Michelle Obama,
or the pastor's wife, one thing is for certain, the
media, both nationally and locally puts great
emphasis on what leaders are wearing. While
certainly there is a standard to uphold, the
clothing is not what makes them the 1st Lady.
What qualifies her for this position is who God
has called her to be. A wife or not, being a
woman of God puts you in a position to
enhance, make better or add value.

You are positioned for greatness. There is nothing small or low level about you. Ditch every negative word that has ever been spoken in your life. You are the first lady of your home and in you is a legacy of grace, elegance and empowerment that will transform your sphere of influence. Do not take lightly the position that God has placed you in. Don't despise your position. God is using it to usher His glory. Yield to him and accept where He has you. Let Him use you on your job, in your community, in your family and in the world. You were anointed for this! There is a grace to do the things He has placed in your heart to do.

You are not off base. You are not out of place. You are right where God wants you. You are in position for an upgrade! God is saying, let me upgrade you my daughter! God is getting ready to take you higher simply by your association with Him. What this means is that He is about to elevate you thus everyone you are connected to will be elevated.

Stay in position!

fAS*h*ONI*s*Ta
PROFILE

QUEEN ESTHER

The Book of Esther

God needed someone who was courageous and brave. He raised Esther to become Queen for such a time. God knew that He would use Esther to make a difference at the right time and place. This also applies to you my dear. God is raising you up for such a time as this. The time is NOW for you to stand high in your stilettos and bolding proclaim the Word of God!

After Esther became Queen she soon found out that there was a plot to kill the Jews. Hearing this Esther step on the scene and took action. Esther called a fast.

"Go, gather together all the Jews who are in Susa, and fast for me. Do not eat or drink for three days, night or day. I and my attendants will fast as you do. When this is done, I will go to the king, even though it is against the law. And if I perish, I perish."

Esther 4:16

Notice here that Esther demonstrated Servant Leadership. She did not ask the people of Susa to do anything that she was not willing to do. She was right there with them. Esther eventually made a move showing the sovereignty of God and His deliverance and protection of the Jews.

ACCE*SS*oRI*z*E
Y O U R   F A I T H

Does your presence add to or deplete situations/relationships?

_____

_____

_____

Are you ready for God to take you to the next level?

_____

_____

_____

_____

What are you doing to prepare you for the next level?

_____

_____

_____

fABuLOUs
FAITH
Time

In your Fabulous "FAITH" Time with God I encourage you to get in His presence. Press in and ask God about your upgrade. Ask Him to upgrade your faith and upgrade your life.

_____
_____
_____
_____
_____
_____
_____
_____
_____
_____
_____
_____
_____
_____
_____
_____
_____
_____
_____
_____
_____
_____

WEEK THREE

"Fashions fade, style is eternal."

— **Yves Saint-Laurent**

AMITRICE LOWE

DAY FIFTEEN

Mrs. Entrepreneur

"She makes linen garments and sells them,
and supplies the merchants with sashes"

Proverbs 31:24

God has given us the power to get wealth. From the beginning God placed Adam and Eve in the Garden of Eden with vegetation and streams of rivers in order to give them exactly what they needed. Throughout the Bible there are many instances where God gives His children strategies to get wealth. In Matthew the 25th chapter, God shows the power of an entrepreneurial spirit.

Matthew 25 shows us that He will multiply that which we are good stewards over. What do you do well? What gifts God has blessed you with that you are just sitting on. How can you turn those gifts into multiple streams of income? How can you become your own boss? As so many women grasp the concept of Matthew 25, they are clocking out of their "9 to 5" and strutting in their God given DESTINY in their 4-inch heels.

Don't overlook the entrepreneur in you. Embrace the skills you have that not only bless your life financially, but also add value to the world around you. If you've been contemplating the entrepreneurial gift on your life, contemplate no more. You don't have to leave your job, but each day strut towards that business. Build what God has put in you and use it for the greater good.

Entrepreneurship looks good on you!

LYDIA

Acts 16:12-15

Lydia was a Christian and an entrepreneur from Thyatira, a city in Turkey. She had influence. Lydia was converted into the Christian Faith (this inspired her household to become Christians) and she opened her home for fellowship as well as she used her resources to help the ministry of God.

Lydia was the maker and seller of purple. Thyatira area waters were adapted for beautiful and permanent dye. Lydia was resourceful and used what was around her to become an entrepreneur, a seller of purple dye, cloth and garments.

ACCESSORIZE
YOUR FAITH

Are you an entrepreneur? If so, are there entrepreneurial qualities you lack that you need to be successful?

_____
_____
_____
_____

🥿 🥿 If not, do you desire to be an
       entrepreneur?

🥿 _____

_____

_____

🥿 How are you using your resources from
   being an entrepreneur to advance the
   Kingdom?

🥿 _____

_____

_____

fABuLOUs
FAITH
Time

In your Fabulous "FAITH" Time with God I
encourage you to get in His presence. Ask God
to unleash the entrepreneur Spirit He has placed
in you. Ask God to give you strategy to get
multiple streams of income so that you can pour

back into the Kingdom.

DAY SIXTEEN
What's In Your Closet

"She is clothed with strength and dignity, and she laughs without fear of the future"

Proverbs 31:25

In speaking with many women they often say, "When I am dressed well I feel better." They go on to say, "When I "feel" good, I perform better!" I'm sure that this may be true but one thing is for sure, we as women of God cannot allow our feelings to dictate the direction of our lives. We have to allow the Word of God and only the Word of God to drive us.

When we know and are rooted in the Word of God, we feel better because of whose God says we are. Knowing what God says about you gives you confidence and you do not have any fear or doubt. This my sister definitely puts you in the best-dressed category.

fASHIONIsTa
PROFILE

THE CHURCH

The church is not the beautiful edifice we go to week after week to worship God. We, both you and I, make up the church. The head of the church is God. In the covenant of marriage with God we (the church) are the weaker vessel, yet we are clothed in strength through Him.

Psalms 93:1 tells us that The LORD reigns, He is clothed with majesty; The LORD has clothed and girded Himself with strength; Indeed, the world is firmly established, it will not be moved. We are clothed in Him and He is our strong tower. As long as we stay in Him then there is no doubt of our future.

✝ACCESSORIZE
Y O U R   F A I T H

🥿 Does what you wear or do not have to
wear dictate how you feel?

🥿_____

_____

_____

🥿 Do you feel knowing the promises of God
for you will help you to be more
confident?

🥿_____

_____

_____

When you feel weak, are you confident in His strength?

_____

_____

_____

fABuLOUs
FAITH
Time

In your Fabulous "FAITH" Time with God I encourage you to get in His presence. Ask God to give you the desire to learn what His promises are for you. Ask God to allow you to only be moved by His Word and not your feelings.

_____
_____
_____
_____
_____
_____
_____
_____
_____
_____
_____
_____
_____
_____
_____
_____
_____
_____
_____
_____
_____
_____
_____

DAY SEVENTEEN

Rip The Runway

"She speaks with wisdom, and faithful instruction is on her tongue"

Proverbs 31:26

"Ms. Amitrice, are you a lawyer," little "Ms. Kate" from Children's Church, asked. I said "No ma'am, why did you ask? She shrugged her shoulders and boldly declared, "I just thought you were a lawyer or something like that." In talking with little Ms. Kate, I realized that our kids are not just listening to us but they are also watching us.

There is an annual hip-hop fashion show where models confidently strut down the run way in the upcoming season of fashion. Ladies, just like the fashion models strut the runway leading us into the season's newest trends, we influence (leading in good things or bad) our children and others by what we say, do and wear. So, I ask: what are we teaching our children?

Did you have the women in the church to come to you and say "Baby pull up your shirt I can see your cleavage?" How about, "It's okay to wear a skirt but it doesn't have to be so short." Have you ever been the one that walked in the church with the short skirt and felt out of place because you can hear and/or see them whispering about you? As I come into contact with many girls and women alike, one thing that I have learned is that everyone did not have a woman of God, a Proverbs Woman, to lead them and show them the things of God.

Being a woman of faith, fashion and fabulous we are commissioned to speak, both verbally and in our actions, wisdom. There is power in mentorship. In your spiritual and professional life you should, if you have not already, identify someone who can speak into your life to help you become better.

fAShIoNIsTa
PROFILE

THE TITUS WOMAN

Titus 2

We are Titus women! Titus women are women who provide Godly mentorship and guidance for the younger women (young here is both young in the natural and in the spirit). When the Titus Woman opens her mouth she speaks out of love and never to tear down. She does not judge, but in love she will correct you. She speaks on those things that are vital to you too becoming a Titus Woman one day.

I have been blessed with many Titus Women in my life, both spiritually and professionally. They correct me when I am wrong and uplift me with Words of encouragement when I need them the most. Minister Williams (a fabulous woman of God) takes simple girly things like applying make-up to help me see the validity of having a solid foundation rooted in God.

✝ACCE*SS*oRIzE
Y O U R   F A I T H

🔖 What are you saying, doing or wearing that may influence a young lady?

🔖 _____

_____

_____

🔖 Are you coachable?

🔖 _____

_____

_____

_____

🩰 Do you have a spiritual mentor/
professional mentor?

🩰 _____

_____

_____

fABuLOUs
FAITH
Time

In your Fabulous "FAITH" Time with God I encourage you
to get in His presence. Ask God to send Titus women to pour
into you. Ask God to help you to become a woman who can
mentor others. Ask God to show you who will be a good fit
for you as a mentor.

_____
_____
_____
_____
_____
_____
_____
_____
_____
_____
_____
_____
_____
_____
_____
_____
_____
_____
_____
_____
_____

AMITRICE LOWE

DAY EIGHTEEN

Gossip Girl

"She looks well to how things go in her household, and the bread of idleness (gossip, discontent, and self-pity) she will not eat."

Proverbs 31:27 (AMP)

"Girl, don't hang with her, she's messy, she talks too much, she's always in other folks business" are words that are used to describe women that are constantly partaking in conversations they shouldn't. In Matthew 12: 36 (NASB) the Word of God states, 'But I tell you that every careless word that people speak, they shall give an accounting for it in the day of judgment." When we as women of God indulge in conversations (whether hearing or listening) and/or say or do things that are not pleasing to God we are partaking in the bread of idleness!

Our words carry so much power and authority. As faith-filled women, we should be good stewards over the direction in which we send our words. Idle talk and gossip brings death to our lives and those around us. We were created to be life-givers and our words should be consistently life giving. Consider your speech and how it impacts the hearts of those you come in contact with. Choose to be the destroyer of gossip and a voice of life each day.

fASHIONIsTa
PROFILE

HANNAH & PENNIAH

1 Samuel 1:1-28

In the book of 1 Samuel it tells a story of two types of women; one who looks well to how things go in her household, and does not eat of the bread of idleness and one who does, Hannah and Penniah. Hannah and Penniah were both wives of Elkanah. Hannah endured being bullied by Penniah. Penniah would be considered a modern day bully, a mean girl, aka "Ms. Rudeness." Penniah tainted and talked about Hannah because she thought that Hannah could not have children while she already had children with Elkanah.

Every year at a time that should have been a joyous occasion, Penniah made the time dreadful for Hannah. Penniah taunted Hannah and Hannah pitied herself because of this. Hannah, being a woman of God, prayed and asked God to give her a son. God eventually allowed her to become pregnant and give birth to Samuel.

Truth is at some point in our lives we may have been a Penniah or better yet, some of us may be showing some Penniah behaviors now. How many times do we invoke ourselves into our girlfriend's business with no intentions of uplifting her, but to bring her down with our words and actions? If you are guilty of this, STOP! We as women of God are commissioned in 1 Thessalonians 5:11to encourage one another and to build each up.

ACCESSORIZE
YOUR FAITH

↳ Are you partaking in the bread of idleness with gossip or other degrading behaviors?

↳ _____

_____

_____

↳ Are you displaying "mean" girls behaviors? Are these behaviors being passed down to your children?

↳ _____

_____

_____

What are some ways you can uplift your peers, friends, people in general?

_____

_____

_____

fABULOUs
FAITH
Time

In your Fabulous "FAITH" Time with God I encourage you to get in His presence. Ask God to show you yourself. Ask Him to fix those areas that are not like you. Ask your Heavenly Father to show you how to uplift people with your words and actions.

AMITRICE LOWE

DAY NINETEEN

Favor Aint Fair

Her children rise up and call her blessed (happy, fortunate, and to be envied); and her husband boasts of *and* praises her, [saying],

Proverbs 31:28 (AMP)

As woman, we may not all be mothers and wives in the natural but one thing that we do have in common is that we loved to be honored. The Bible clearly instructs us to give honor where honor is due. All of us ladies can think of the one person that raised us from a child to womanhood and deem them worthy to be honored because of the many sacrifices that was made on our behalf.

Likewise, a coworker, a friend or family member honor us on our birthday it makes us feel appreciated, it makes us feel happy, blessed and loved. Many of us will also agree that we can honor our love ones in our actions and behaviors. A thought to ponder: In deed or words, have you honored your love ones today?

MARY

The angel went to Mary and said, "Greetings, you who are highly favored! The Lord is with you." Mary, when told that she had been sought after by God to carry The King of Kings, did not feel worthy because she was worried about what other would say. Mary didn't feel unworthy, but she simply surrendered to the plan and Mary was honored for this. Jesus was made proud and honored her. When Mary asked Jesus to turn water into wine, He honored her request. Even at the time of His crucifixion, Jesus honored her making sure that someone was left behind to care for her.

ACCESSORIZE
YOUR FAITH

Are you living a lifestyle that is worthy of honor with your family, friends, and/or colleagues?

_____

_____

_____

_____

🥿 Do you feel appreciate by family and
friends?

🥿 _____

_____

_____

🥿 When/If honored (in word or action) do
you discount it because you secretly do not
feel worthy?

🥿 _____

_____

_____

fABuLOUs
FAITH
Time

In your Fabulous "FAITH" Time with God I encourage you to get in His presence. Ask God do you have feelings of unworthiness and therefore you discount compliments and gestures that are designed to honor you. Ask God are you living in a way that is worth honor. Ask Him to speak to you about what you can do to live an honorable life.

_____
_____
_____
_____
_____
_____
_____
_____
_____
_____
_____
_____
_____
_____
_____
_____
_____
_____
_____
_____
_____
_____
_____

DAY TWENTY

The Phenomenal Woman

Many daughters have done virtuously, but thou
excellest them all."

Proverbs 31:29

To be virtuous is to be morally excellent. Are you
looking for acceleration? Acceleration is the
benefit of excellence. We are propelled into new
realms of greatness through our willingness to let
God maximize our full potential. When we live
life "full on" with God we are not just virtuous,
but phenomenal.

Virtue is what you are made to be and in and
through God, you are not only virtuous but you
are equipped to go beyond the ordinary. God
made woman not just to have a good life, but
also to have a great life of abundance.

Proverbs 31:29 encourages us to live the fabulous life as a woman of God. In the New Testament of the Bible Jesus declares that He will leave us someone that will dwell on the inside of us that will empower us to be the woman of Heavenly Father called us to be.

The Holy Spirit that lives on the inside of you is one powerful tool. It gives you the "dunmas" power you need to be the phenomenal woman you were fashioned to be. God is our accelerator and He is pushes us into excellence. Don't settle for ordinary when God calls you excellent.

fAS*h*ioNIs**T**a
PROFILE

ANNA
Luke 2:36-38

Phenomenal is the word to describe someone who consistently lived face to face with God, Anna. Anna devoted her life to God. She served Him whole-heartedly. The Bible tells us that Anna never left the temple. She worshiped night and day, fasting and praying and continuously gave thanks. Ladies, we can have the same phenomenal life as Anna. We too can be so devoted to God that we pray without ceasing and give God thanks in all things.

ACCE*SS*oRI*z*E
Y O U R   F A I T H

Are you living a virtuous life?

_____

_____

_____

Are you committed to serving God with your whole heart?

_____

_____

_____

_____

🥿 Are you fasting and praying on a consistent basis?

🥿 _____

_____

_____

fABuLoUs
FAITH
Time

In your Fabulous "FAITH" Time with God I encourage you to get in His presence. Ask God to give you the desire to want more of Him.

_____
_____
_____
_____
_____
_____
_____
_____
_____
_____
_____
_____
_____
_____
_____
_____
_____
_____
_____
_____
_____

DAY TWENTY-ONE
Beauty is Her Name

"Charm is deceitful and beauty is vain, *But* a woman who fears the LORD, she shall be praised."

Proverbs 31:30

True beauty comes from within. There is a contemporary gospel song that declares, "The joy I feel on the inside will show up on the outside." Merian Webster defines charm as something that is believed to have magic powers. The scripture above states that charm is deceitful. Deceitful is defined as being misleading and fraudulent.

Here we see that the act of charming is misleading and fraudulent and beauty is vain. Girl, the Word of God is telling us that although we like to dress nice and smell good, do not boast about and become prideful about our outward appearance. If we focus more on our physical we have missed it. What God has placed on the inside is what yields outward beauty. A woman who fears (fear here is to reverence God) God in her appearance and abilities shall be praised.

fAS/lONIsTa
PROFILE

SARAH
(FORMALLY KNOWN AS SARAI)
Genesis Chapter 17

Sarah was beautiful and her husband knew it. Though Sarah had an outward beauty, she had some internal struggles. Sarah was much like us, she had a struggle with patience. In the 17th chapter of Genesis and the 17th verse God made Abraham and Sarah a promise: I will bless her, and indeed I will give you a son by her. Then I will bless her, and she shall be *a mother of* nations.

When Sarah heard this promise she laughed. Sarah laughed because she was old and she thought she was too old to have a son. Sarah did as we often do, intervene in God's business because we do not see immediate manifestation. Sarah got distracted by her natural situation and decided to take matters into her own hands.

Sarah allowed her maid to sleep with her husband and this turn into a disaster. Ultimately God's plan prevailed, as He promised, and Sarah gave birth to Isaac. Ladies, remember we should always be in a position of reverence to God because God is the one constant person we know! When God makes a covenant with us He is sure to keep it, just trust Him!

✝ACCESSORIZE
Y O U R   F A I T H

🥿 What has God promised you that has not yet manifested?

🥿 _____

_____

_____

🥿 Have you allowed your natural situation to get in the way of His "SUPER" natural PROMISE?

🥿 _____

_____

_____

_____

How can you practice patience while awaiting the promise to manifest?

_____

_____

_____

fABuLOUs
FAITH
Time

In your Fabulous "FAITH" Time with God I encourage you to get in His presence. In this time soak in His presence and think on the things that He has promised you. Ask God to keep you from intervening in His plan.

Honor her for all that her hands have done, and
let her works bring her praise at the city gate.
Proverbs 31:31(NIV)

Congratulations are in order! You have step into
a more faithful and fabulous YOU! Twenty-one
days ago you (alone or with your girls) joined me
on a journey into the lives of some trailblazing
Fashionistas. Some of the women provided great
examples of what to do and others not so
noteworthy, nonetheless, their life story helped
increase our faith as women of God.

When we first took this step I mentioned that
this was a book for the woman that wants it all.
YOU determine what is "ALL". Being honest,
sometimes we as women are indecisive about
what "all" is for us. If this is you I want to
encourage you and let you know that God has

already placed YOUR all in you. Before God placed you in your mother's womb He placed vision, destiny and purpose in you (Jeremiah 29:11)! Hopefully now your faith is at a level where you are ready to give birth spiritually. You are ready to push out greater faith, a new mindset, a new career, business, house, car, etc.

For those of you that have given birth in the natural you know that when you are ready to give birth the doctors and the nurses are there to help you push. Just as the midwives like Shiphrah and Puah were there to help the women push out great leaders such as Moses. God is sending midwives your way to coach you as you push out Greatness! PUSH! Scream if you have to, PUSH! Cry if you have to! Just PUSH out the vision God has birthed in you!

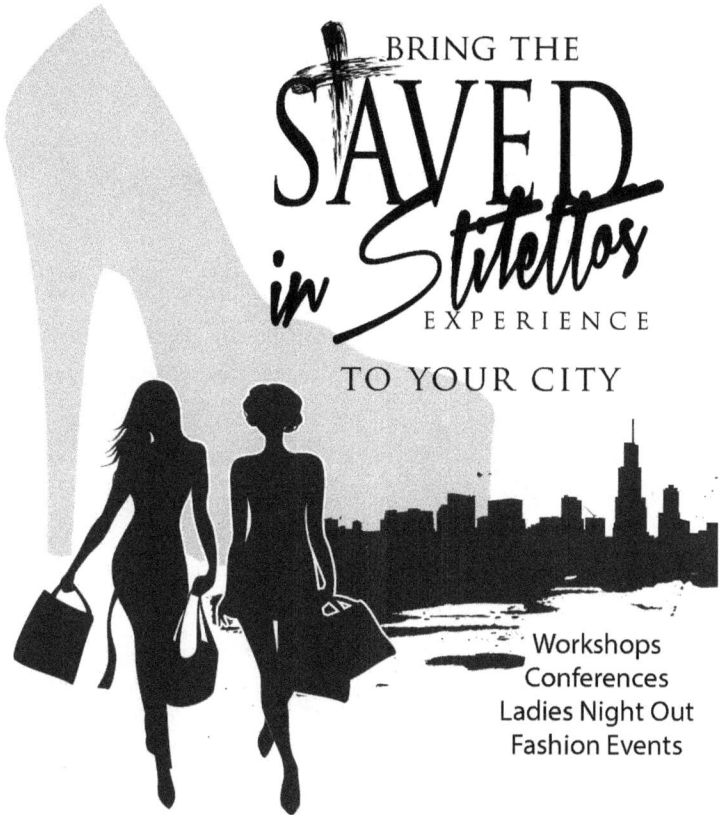

BRING THE SAVED in Stilettos EXPERIENCE TO YOUR CITY

Workshops
Conferences
Ladies Night Out
Fashion Events

e-mail: amlowe77@hotmail.com

ABOUT THE AUTHOR

Amitrice Lowe is a community outreach professional with a heart for empowering women to discover and embrace their greatness in God. With a passion for teaching & creativity she uses her God-given gifts to inspire, encourage and edify the world around her. As CEO of Devine Bling, a custom design t-shirt company and Saved In Stilettos Ministries, Amitrice holds a B.S. in Business Administration and a Masters of Public Administration from Columbus State University. She resides in Columbus, Georgia with her two children